THE SECOND LIFE OF TREES

Aimée M. Bissonette

illustrated by
Nic Jones

Albert Whitman & Company
Chicago, Illinois

Coniferous trees have cones as well as narrow leaves called needles. Most coniferous trees are evergreen trees, which keep their needles all year.

In a forest on the shores of a lake, stands an old evergreen tree, a balsam fir. Its needles are thick, dark, and green. Its bark is rough—ridged with dried resin. The tree is not alone. It is surrounded.

Boreal forests, with coniferous and deciduous trees, are the northernmost in the world. Winters are long; summers are short and cool.

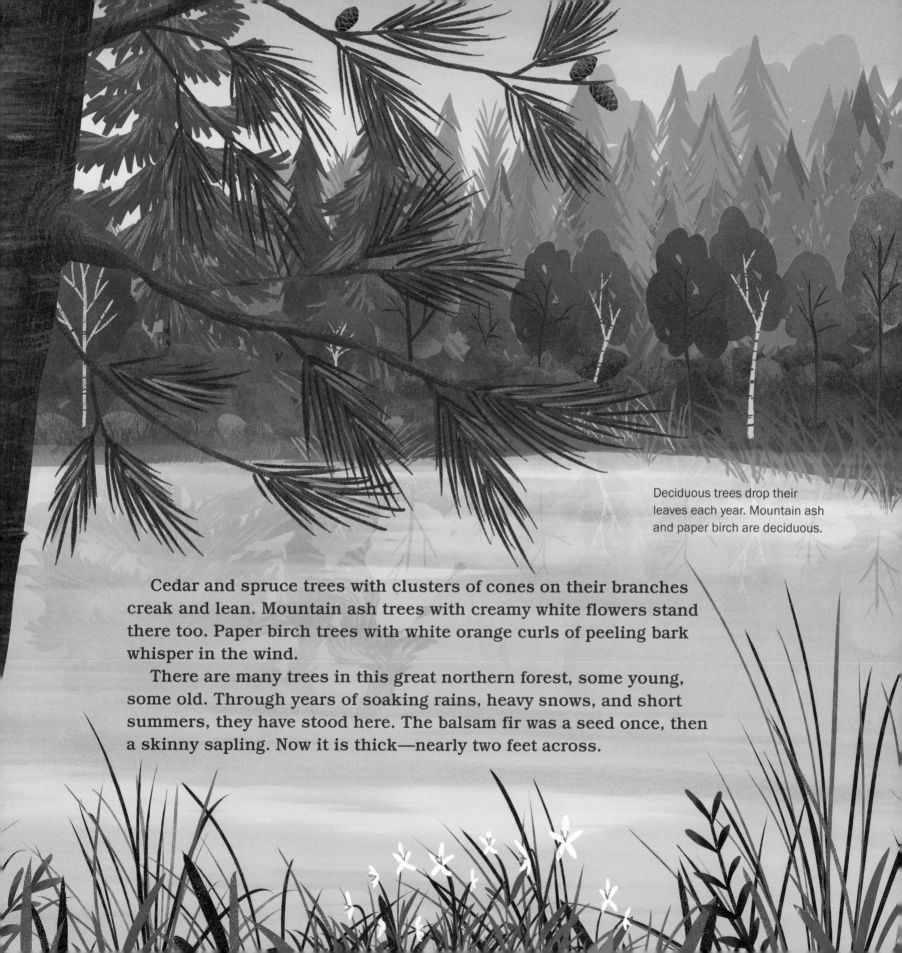

Deciduous trees drop their leaves each year. Mountain ash and paper birch are deciduous.

Cedar and spruce trees with clusters of cones on their branches creak and lean. Mountain ash trees with creamy white flowers stand there too. Paper birch trees with white orange curls of peeling bark whisper in the wind.

There are many trees in this great northern forest, some young, some old. Through years of soaking rains, heavy snows, and short summers, they have stood here. The balsam fir was a seed once, then a skinny sapling. Now it is thick—nearly two feet across.

Chickadees, tiny birds that stay all winter instead of flying south to a warmer climate, live in the balsam fir. They nest inside hollows lined with moss, animal hair, and feathers. Some chickadees dig their own nests; others use holes left by woodpeckers. The tree gives them shelter and a bounty of insect food.

Chickadees eat seeds, insects, insect eggs, and insect larvae (young insects). They pry open tree bark with their bills, so they find plenty of food in the boreal forest.

Red squirrels are sometimes called pine squirrels, or chickarees. They eat mainly conifer seeds, but they also eat mushrooms.

Chattering red squirrels race up and down the tree's trunk. They leap among the branches, snacking on seeds and cones. If the weather turns bad, they snuggle deep into the tree's soft needles.

Deer, moose, and rabbits shelter beneath the tree in bad weather. The tree's dense branches help block wind, rain, and snow.

Owls roost within the tree, and eagles perch high atop it, watching for fish in lake waters below.

For some animals, the balsam fir is dinner itself: budworms eat the tree's branch tips, and chipmunks eat the tree's seeds and bark.

And in springtime, black bears strip its sapwood, the tree's newly formed outer wood, to eat the green wood underneath.

All this snacking can weaken a tree.

But the tree stands tall. It has been here for decades, a place of nesting and resting, safety and food.

The spruce budworm is one of the most destructive insects native to boreal forests. It defoliates, or eats away at, a tree's leaves before the tree is ready to lose them, sometimes causing trees to die.

The tree does even more than provide shelter and food. It filters pollution. It changes carbon dioxide, a gas in the air, to oxygen, a gas we all need to breathe. It slows water runoff on the ground during heavy rains, keeping the soil from washing away. Trees are important to people too.

Leaves soak up water and carbon dioxide. Tiny green grains called chlorophyll help the leaves use the sun's energy to turn water and gas into sugars that trees need to grow. The trees then also release oxygen. This whole process is called photosynthesis.

Trees take up gases that they need to grow from the soil, through their roots. When trees die, their leaves and branches soften and break down, so the nutrients return to the soil. They then feed other plants and animals.

Trees do not last forever.

Some trees are lost to fire: surface fires that move along the forest floor, burning leaf litter and fallen branches; understory fires with waves licking up the trunks of trees; intense crown fires spurred on by the wind, which skip from treetop to treetop, burning all the trees in the stand.

The hot, dry conditions created by global warming—high temperatures, early snow melt, and dry soil—are making these fires worse.

Some trees are lost to insect invasion—whole forests of ash, elm, and chestnut trees across the United States; hundreds of thousands of beech trees in Germany; miles and miles of fir, pine, and spruce trees in Siberia.

All over the world, hungry insects bore holes into trees. They eat the tree's leaves, bark, and soft insides. They lay eggs in the trees, which leads to more bugs and more damage.

And with the insects comes disease. Insects carry germs into the trees. Some germs enter trees through the pits and cracks made by the insects. Disease attacks trees across the globe. It has wiped out olive groves in Italy; sickened elm forests in Canada; and caused limbs to fall off African baobab trees.

In Italy a disease carried by sap-sucking insects such as spittlebugs has caused great damage to olive trees and, as a result, to the country's jobs and economy.

Some trees are lost to the weather. Even the oldest, biggest trees are at the mercy of the weather.

One day the wind howls and waves pound the shore. Rain pours down. Lightning flashes. The balsam fir's roots cannot hold.

WHOOSH! WHOMP! SMASH!

The tree crashes to the ground.

When a tree is uprooted, a large mass of roots and soil, called a root wad, is ripped from the ground. The uprooting is called tree throw or wind throw.

Roots anchor a tree to the earth, stopping the tree from tipping over, but winds put a lot of sideways pressure on trees. In strong storms, young trees often snap; old trees may be uprooted.

Is that all there is? Has the tree's long life ended? It is easy to think the tree's time has passed.

But there is more to this story. This tree hasn't stopped giving. The forest still needs this tree. Its second life starts now.

Changes start with activity so small it's not even visible. You cannot see the tiny living creatures called bacteria, but they are first on the scene. They get to work right away, breaking down the fibers that make up the tree's wood. But bacteria don't act alone. They are part of a team.

As soon as a tree falls, it starts to soften and break apart. Bacteria, insects, and fungi such as mold and mushrooms form a team of recyclers that help chew and crush the tree's wood until it crumbles.

Next come bark beetles that bore holes in the wood, carving paths in the tree's surface. Piles of fine sawdust show where they work. Other insects, millipedes, and spiders follow. They munch and crunch and soften the wood.

Rows of mushrooms grow on the fallen tree's bark. They shred and splinter the wood as they dig in and grow.

Carpenter ants chew their way in and nest inside the tree. They grind the wood into a powder until the tree weakens and sags.

Bark beetles are excellent decomposers. Mature bark beetles and their larvae tunnel into fallen trees and eat the wood.

Earthworms eat the bacteria and fungi. They break down the deadwood even more, turning it into a soil called humus, good for new plant growth.

Spring rains fill the hole in the earth where the tree was uprooted. It's a new source of water for forest animals and birds. Frogs, toads, and newts are drawn to the soft, soggy soil. Spotted salamanders with sticky tongues come, too, searching for pill bugs and snails.

Flowers spring up around the tree. Its second life continues. Delicate blossoms of trout lilies, fairy spuds, Dutchman's-breeches, and columbine spread among lacy ferns and surround the tree like a blanket. Yellow, pink, and red blooms dot the forest floor.

The floor of a boreal forest is usually covered with mosses, ferns, and wildflowers.

Nuthatches and spring warblers flock to the tree for insect dinners. Woodpeckers drill at the bark, tossing wood chunks into the air. By summer these birds have created small hollows—safe, new resting places for mice and shrews.

Lizards and snakes love the tree's cracks and crannies. They slip under its bark whenever danger is near. The tree, now in its second life, hums with activity—animals nesting and looking for food.

The cavities created by woodpeckers are used as homes by many animals and birds, including bluebirds, flycatchers, small owls, porcupines, bats, and rodents.

Songbirds eat as many as 300 insects a day during the summer. Many of these insects damage living trees, so songbirds are important for keeping a forest healthy.

More animals come. The tree has so many uses! The animals use nearly every part of the fallen tree in every stage of its decay. A red fox lounges on it, soaking up sun. Chipmunks and red squirrels use the tree as a speedway, racing down its long length above the cluttered forest floor.

Experts estimate that two-thirds of all wildlife species use dead and fallen trees during some portion of their life cycles.

Trees that fall into streams and ponds have a second life too. Turtles and beavers use them as sun perches. Fishers, mink, ducks, and other birds hunt from them. Fish, frogs, and crustaceans use fallen trees as places to hide and breed.

When late fall arrives, mammals seek shelter. Ermine choose the tree for their den, packing an abandoned hollows with beds of plants and fur. A black bear settles into the tree's tangle of roots. It feasts on ants as it prepares for a long winter's sleep.

When winter winds bury the tree in cold snow drifts, all is quiet, but the forest dwellers are there. Wood frogs lie in frozen sleep beneath the leaf litter. Bees shelter within the log, as do butterflies. Hungry mice scurry back and forth through icy mouse tunnels beneath the snow. They come for seeds they stashed in the tree's nooks and crannies and underneath the log before winter.

The ants that crawl over, under, and through fallen trees are an important food source for bears.

Season after season, the tree keeps on giving. How long it lasts depends on so many things. Is it made of hardwood or softwood? How wet is the weather? How tall was the tree, and how thick was its trunk?

As the tree crumbles, it offers food, protection, and living spaces for many—animal, insect, and bird. Until at last, there is nothing left to hold it together. It becomes part of the soil, returning the lifetime of goodness it took from the earth.

How long it takes for a fallen tree to completely decompose is called residence time. The residence time for softwood trees such as evergreens is from 55–125 years. Hardwood trees take from 45–70 years to break down.

Fallen trees that have been on
the forest floor often look solid
but may be decomposing and full
of activity within.

It is then, at the end of the tree's second life, that a wondrous thing happens. A small sprig of green shoots up from what is left of the tree. It starts as a seed and grows into a sapling. It stretches up toward the sun shining down through the leaves.

A nurse log is a fallen tree that has decomposed, making the surrounding soil richer and creating a place for new seeds to sprout and take root.

Seeds driven by the wind collect on nurse logs. So do seeds carried there from animals like mice, moles, and voles that stash seeds in the tree for winter food.

When seedlings sprout on a nurse log, their roots thicken and creep down and around the log to the soil. In time, the roots become strong and thick enough to support the seedling, and a new tree grows.

Nature is the world's best recycler. The tree in its second life has given one final gift. The small sprig of green is at the start of its journey. The forest needs this new tree. Life starts again.

Dead and dying trees in a forest are not a sign that the forest is sick. Healthy forests depend on the death of trees to bring new life to the forest.

Author's Note

Ever since I was a little girl I have loved the woods. I hike in the spring, summer, and fall. I snowshoe in the winter. The woods smell wonderful and there is so much to see.

Whether I am in a forest, a state park, or at the local nature center, I always look at the trees: uprooted trees, standing trees with hollows, and broken trees or "snags." Perhaps you look for them too.

Foresters used to clear dead and broken trees away. They wanted to keep their forests tidy and were worried that too much deadwood could lead to forest fires. They did not realize that trees have such an active "second life." In recent years, researchers have shown that leaving fallen trees and branches, as well as standing dead trees, is incredibly important to plants, wildlife, and the overall health of the forest.

What pleases me about trees is that I almost always spy wildlife when I see them—squirrels racing around tree trunks and diving into cavities; thick, beautiful staircases of mushrooms running the length of a fallen log; spring warblers on windy days who fly down and land on fallen trees in search of insect meals; and my favorite, a lazy red fox lying atop a sunny log, keeping an eye on me as I walk past.

Trees—both living and dead—are microhabitats where all sorts of activity takes place. All you need to do is stop and look. Dead trees are not lifeless. They are awash with wildlife every season of the year.

Exploring Snags and Fallen Logs

Next time you walk in the woods, take some time to study the trees. Look for trees with hollows, snags, and fallen logs. Can you find some? If so, here are some questions to consider:

- What do you think happened to the tree or log? How did it die?
- What is living on the tree or log? Do you see moss, fungi, or insects?
- Do you see evidence of woodpeckers? What does that look like?
- If you are by a stream or pond and come across a fallen tree, do you see insects or fish? Is the tree affecting the flow of the water?
- Touch the wood of a dead tree. How does it feel? Moist or dry?
- Is the bark loose? Is it lying on the ground?
- Can you lift the log or gently roll it over? What is living underneath?
- How long ago do you think the tree died?

Additional Reading

Ambrose, Jamie. *Woodland and Forest: Explore Nature with Fun Facts and Activities*. New York: DK, 2017.

Pfeffer, Wendy. *A Log's Life*. New York: Simon & Schuster, 1997.

Twiddy, Robin. *Rot and Mold*. New York: Kidhaven, 2019.

Van Gageldonk, Mack. *All About Forests*. New York: Clavis, 2016.

Wohlleben, Peter. *Can You Hear the Trees Talking? Discovering the Hidden Life of the Forest*. Vancouver, BC: Greystone, 2019.

For Aliza, who loves the forests of the Upper Peninsula as much as I do—
and of course, with love to Bryan, Maureen, and Brian—AMB

Forever my babies, Mia, Aeran, and Ander—NJ

Library of Congress Cataloging-in-Publication data is on file with the publisher.
Text copyright © 2021 Aimée M. Bissonette
Illustrations copyright © 2021 by Albert Whitman & Company
Illustrations by Nic Jones
Thank you to Anastasiia Drakova for the additonal artwork.
First published in the United States of America in 2021 by Albert Whitman & Company

ISBN 978-0-8075-7281-8 (hardcover)
ISBN 978-0-8075-7282-5 (ebook)

Printed in China

10 9 8 7 6 5 4 3 2 1 WKT 26 25 24 23 22 21

Design by Rick DeMonico

For more information about Albert Whitman & Company,
visit our website at www.albertwhitman.com.